The British Liberal Tradition:
From Gladstone to Young Churchill,
Asquith, and Lloyd George –
Is Blair Their Heir?

Lord Roy Jenkins

The British Liberal Tradition

From Gladstone to Young Churchill, Asquith, and Lloyd George – Is Blair Their Heir?

LORD ROY JENKINS

Published in association with
Victoria University by
University of Toronto Press

© University of Toronto Press Incorporated 2001
Toronto Buffalo London
Printed in Canada

ISBN 0-8020-8454-0

Printed on acid-free paper

The Senator Keith Davey Lectures

National Library of Canada Cataloguing in Publication Data

Jenkins, Roy
The British liberal tradition : from Gladstone to young
Churchill, Asquith, and Lloyd George – is Blair their heir?

(The Senator Keith Davey lectures)
ISBN 0-8020-8454-0

1. Liberal Party (Great Britain) – History.   2. Liberalism –
Great Britain – History.   3. Great Britain – Politics and
government – 1837–1901.   4. Great Britain – Politics and
government – 20th century.   I. Title.   II. Series: Senator
Keith Davey lecture series.

JN1129.L45J46 2001   324.24106'09   C2001-930247-9

University of Toronto Press acknowledges the financial
assistance to its publishing program of the Canada Council
for the Arts and the Ontario Arts Council.

University of Toronto Press acknowledges the financial
support for its publishing activities of the Government of
Canada through the Book Publishing Industry Development
Program (BPIDP).

Contents

THE FOURTH ANNUAL SENATOR KEITH DAVEY LECTURE

CONCLUDING REMARKS

BIOGRAPHICAL NOTES

Preface

H.G. Wells wrote that 'history is a race between catastrophe and education.' When one has had the privilege of listening to and reading a wonderful lecture like this one which was delivered by Lord Jenkins, one has the impression, however fleeting, that education is winning. I would like to thank all those who were present and all those who have purchased this slim volume, for contributing to that victory.

We have more than one winning score to celebrate. I heard that wagers were being taken on whether this lecture would, once again, be delivered in a snowstorm. The clement weather made and lost more than one minor fortune.

This is not the first time that some people have been misled in similar circumstances. When Churchill came to the United States, he took the train to Missouri with President Truman. Churchill asked if they might play cards, mentioning that he had once played poker in the Boer War. Truman acquiesced and instructed his staff to play their best. He was certain that Churchill was just being a model of British modesty. After Churchill began losing seriously, Truman reconsidered and countermanded his initial order. He said that, as a courtesy to the guest, the staff should play poorly, allowing Churchill to win. Today Mother Nature has allowed us to win.

To continue with Truman, he once said that 'men make history – history does not make the man.' Well, Senator Davey has consistently made history in Canada. His successes have truly been remarkable, and they have been accomplished thanks to a strong team effort with his wife Dorothy. I salute them both.

I would like to thank Dean Beach of the Faculty of Music for allowing us to use its hall and the members of the organizing committee for their fine work: Ms Stephanie Connolly, Senator and Mrs Davey, Dr Paul Fox, Dr Brian

Merrilees, Mr Corey Salih, and Dr Rob Vipond.

I am also deeply indebted to Sir Anthony Goodenough, the High Commissioner for Great Britain in Canada and the co-host of Lord Jenkins's lecture. He brought with him Baroness Scotland of Asthal, Minister for the Americas in the British Cabinet, and Mr Tony Curren, British Consul General in Toronto.

The previous year's lecture was co-hosted by Mr Heinrich Kroon, Consul General of the Netherlands, who attended this year. On the same day as Lord Jenkins spoke we were proud to launch the publication of the third lecture in our series, *Revitalizing Liberal Values in a Globalizing World*, by Dr Ruud Lubbers, former Prime Minister of the Netherlands.

I would like to thank the Provost of the University of Toronto for accepting to speak at Lord Jenkins's lecture. We are fortunate to have such a fine scholar and academic leader with excellent administrative skills. It would be very hard indeed to imagine a better Provost.

Lord Jenkins was introduced by the Honorable H.N.R. Jackman, Chancellor of the University of Toronto and distinguished Victoria graduate. One of the qualifications of the person selected to introduce Lord Jenkins was that he or she had to have read all of Jenkins's books. Fortunately, our Chancellor is a history buff, and not only had he already read these books, but he also had already had the pleasure of meeting Lord Jenkins.

Lord Jenkins was thanked at the event by columnist Richard Gwyn. Churchill said that 'the empires of the future are the empires of the mind.' Mr Gwyn's writing is an illustration of a superb mind at work. His words were not recorded and therefore could not be included in this volume. However, we do have the delightful toast that was proposed by Mr H. Garfield Emerson, President and CEO of N.M. Rothschild and Sons Canada Limited. Mr Emerson is well known for his leadership in the world of business and is a remarkable graduate of both Victoria University and the Faculty of Law.

We were also especially fortunate to welcome Baroness Scotland, who shared with us her reflections on the lecture and on relations between Canada and Great Britain.

In concluding my prefatory remarks, I remind you of what Churchill said at the Battle of Egypt, 'This is not the end. Nor is it the beginning of the end.' It may, however, be the end of the beginning. So, let us proceed to the lecture!

Roseann Runte
President
Victoria University

Introductory Remarks

Opening Comment

ADEL SEDRA
Provost, University of Toronto

I am very honoured to welcome everyone on behalf of the University of Toronto.

I would like to extend an especially warm welcome to Senator Davey and his wife Dorothy. Thank you for lending your prestigious name to this lecture series. Events such as these lectures are very important to the intellectual life of the University of Toronto. Our university has always enjoyed a tremendously rich liberal arts tradition and fosters opportunities for growth outside the classroom. This is an aspiration we share with Victoria University. Victoria is well known for its vibrant tradition of humanism and scholarship. Victoria has produced many graduates who have gone on to distinguished public service. It is very fitting, therefore, that Victoria University has chosen Lord Jenkins to deliver this year's Senator Keith Davey lecture.

Lord Jenkins, we are honoured that a scholar and a statesman of your renown is this year's speaker. I look forward to hearing the words and wisdom of someone who has had such a highly successful career in the public and academic arenas. On this side of the Atlantic, we have always watched with interest – and sometimes puzzlement – the changes that Britain has undergone over the past century. I am sure this lecture will deepen our understanding of your wonderful country and its fascinating political history.

Introduction

THE HONORABLE
H.N.R. JACKMAN
Chancellor, University of Toronto

It is my honour to present to you Lord Roy Jenkins, Baron of Pontypool in the County of Gwent. Lord Jenkins is Chancellor of Oxford University. He is a man of many talents and diverse interests.

It is no surprise that the author of some seventeen books is President of the Royal Society of Literature. Nor is it surprising that the first President of the European Community is now co-President of the Royal Institute of International Affairs. Nor is it extraordinary that the first leader of the Social Democratic Party is now the leader of the Social and Liberal peers. What is extraordinary is that all of these functions have been so admirably filled by the same person. When we speak today of multi-tasking, it might have been Lord Jenkins who inspired this term.

Lord Jenkins comes from a distinguished family of political leaders. His father was Arthur Jenkins, M.P. Lord Jenkins is a graduate of University College, Cardiff, and Balliol College, Oxford. After serving in the war from 1939 to 1946, and a decade in business, he became a Member of Parliament for Central Southwark in 1948, and was soon personal private secretary to the Secretary of State for Commonwealth Relations, then Minister of Aviation, Home Secretary, Chancellor of the Exchequer, Deputy Leader of the Labour Party, and President of the European Community. He was then elected as a Social Democratic MP and served as the U.K. Delegate to the Council of Europe. He was also President of the 'Britain in Europe' referendum campaign.

Lord Jenkins holds many honours, among which are the Order of Merit from Britain, the Order of European Merit, the Grand Cross, the Legion of Honour of Senegal, the Legion of Honour of Mali, the Order of Charles III

(Spain), the Order of Merit (Italy), and the Order of Infante D. Henrique (Portugal). He has received many honorary degrees and numerous prizes.

Among his many award-winning books are *Gladstone*, *A Life at the Centre*, *Asquith*, *Afternoon on the Potomac*, *What Matters Now*, *Nine Men of Power*, *Partnership of Principle*, *Truman*, *Baldwin*, *Gallery of Twentieth-Century Portraits*, *Pursuit of Progress*, and *Mr. Balfour's Poodle*.

Lord Jenkins has been writing a biography of Churchill, and I understand that this lecture is a special preview of his findings.

I had the privilege of meeting Lord Jenkins in England earlier this year and I am now delighted to share that privilege with you.

The Fourth Annual
Senator Keith Davey Lecture

The British Liberal Tradition

From Gladstone to Young Churchill, Asquith, and Lloyd George – Is Blair Their Heir?

LORD ROY JENKINS
Chancellor, Oxford University

It is a great pleasure to me to pay what I think is my seventh visit to the city of Toronto, but my first for nearly four years; and to speak under the auspices of Victoria University but within the territory of the University of Toronto. As Chancellor of Oxford I am closely familiar with the complicated – sometimes delicate, but on the whole amicable – relations between free-standing colleges. We have thirty-nine of them, varying in age between 750 and 10 years – and varying in wealth, too – and an overarching but far from all-powerful university.

I am also delighted to be asked to give the Keith Davey lecture, which already in its four years of existence has achieved a considerable reputation – and not only for snowstorms. I have given quite a lot of named lectures, but only very rarely with the pleasure but also the challenge of having the eponymous figure present and sitting in the middle of the first row. I think the last occasion was when I gave a George Ball lecture at Princeton, in the presence of that powerful personality who, of all the major U.S. foreign policy advisers in the days of the so-called Imperial Presidency, had the distinction of being almost invariably (so I thought) on the right side. Senator Keith Davey is in that position today, and I am honoured that he and his wife are here.

Now this is essentially a historical lecture, centred around the figures named in the somewhat cumbersome title. It is the story of the rise and fall of the British Liberal Party as a governing party, with a final section on where Tony Blair stands in relation to the Liberal tradition. There may be some lessons for Canadian politics in the story, but if there are, I leave it to you to draw them. I have always found it unwise to ·lecture an audience on a subject about which they manifestly know more than I do.

I think, however, that I ought to give you a few introductory words on my own political position. I have always been a liberal with a small 'l', but I am proud today to call myself a Liberal with a capital 'L' as well – a Liberal Democrat, of the party that was formed in 1987 by amalgamation with the SDP, made up mainly of those who had come out of the Labour Party in 1981 and had already fought three general elections in close alliance with the old Liberal Party. We are a party with a very strong base in local government – cities and counties – plus 46 seats in the House of Commons. And over the last four general elections we have polled an average of around 20 per cent of the popular vote.

The Liberal Party was born at a meeting in Willis's Rooms, St James's, London, on the afternoon of the 6th of June, 1859. It was an odd place for the accouchement of what was to be a largely nonconformist, even in many ways a puritanical party, for Willis's Rooms, was, as its name implies, a faintly rakish locale. It was the successor to Almack's, a fine haunt of early nineteenth-century gambling and general dissipation. Furthermore, among the 274 MPs and many members of the House of Lords who

were present, there were several Whig mag-
nates, who could easily have accommodated
the whole lot in their own London house. And
there was also the Reform Club, built to
Charles Barry's palatial design only sixteen
years before, and then – as it no longer is –
politically partisan, which would have been
more than adequately welcoming. But Willis's
Rooms it was. And what there took place had a
remarkable impact on the political life of Britain for at least the next six decades. In this context it was the equivalent of Martin Luther
nailing his notice to the church door in Witten-
berg, or of the embattled farmers by the rood
bridge at Lexington firing 'the shot heard
round the world.'

Of the six (or maybe seven) Liberal prime
ministers of the next sixty years, the first two,
Palmerston and Lord John Russell, were
present at the creation. Indeed, by their somewhat pro forma expressions of mutual respect,
they made the occasion, to which John Bright,
a greater orator than a minister, also contrib-
uted. Another three future prime ministers –
Rosebery, Campbell-Bannerman, and Asquith
– were not present for the good reason that
they were respectively aged twelve, twenty-

three, and six at the time. Nor was Lloyd George, who was aged minus four, and who in any event was a somewhat doubtful member of the sextet or septet, for although he was a prime minister – and a most notable one – who was a Liberal, he never presided over a Liberal government, and indeed did a great deal to break the Liberal Party as an instrument of government. But the most surprising absentee was Gladstone, who was the greatest beneficiary of the event, and who in his four premierships was the dominant Liberal figure of the remaining forty-one years of the nineteenth century. He deliberately stood back.

Gladstone, who in my view was undoubtedly the greatest British prime minister of the nineteenth century, just as Churchill was of the twentieth, had not of course started his long political career, spanning sixty-three years in the House of Commons, as a Liberal. Indeed, he had been referred to in 1839 by Thomas Babington Macaulay famously and somewhat satirically as 'the rising hope of those stern and unbending Tories.' But he became a key figure in the 1841 to 1846 government of Sir Robert Peel, which was nominally Conservative, although not nearly enough so for Disraeli, who made his name by splitting from Peel, although at the price of making the Conservative Party very nearly unelectable for twenty years. Peel did a great deal to lay the foundations of Liberal England. At the beginning of the Peel government, Britain was far from being the stable and prosperous parliamentary semi-democracy of the middle and late Victorian period. Chartist agitation was at its height in the couple of years before the Peel government came in, and Britain was regarded as just as potentially eruptive a society as France, which bracketed those years with revolutions in 1830 and 1848. Britain was also still suffering from a long, post–Napoleonic Wars depression, and her public finances were in an appalling state. Interest on debt accounted for half the budget, and the other half was substantially made up by the payment of a great number of sinecure salaries. Her revenue – admittedly only £47 million – came from a vast spread of over 750 mostly illogical customs and excise duties. The Peel reforms not only repealed the Corn Laws – which led to the split with Disraeli and other old-guard Conservatives – but also cleared up a good deal of the mess and gave Britain the opportunity to be the major free-trade/free-market industrial power of the world. And it made the third quarter of the nineteenth century – in complete contrast with the second quarter – the period of Britain's most unchallenged industrial supremacy in the world, and with a marked spreading of quiet, unostentatious prosperity and greater political calm. It was also a period unsullied by the imperial pretension and showiness of the fourth quarter of the century. There was no tendency to imperial braggadocio or expansionary wars in the post-Peel third quarter. Indeed, the tendency was to reduce imperial commitments, as in the British North America Act of 1867 – the first major move toward self-government and the surrender of power within the British Empire.

Gladstone was an adjutant of and the heir to Peel. He was left a powerful but uprooted politician throughout the 1850s. He was powerful because of his phenomenal energy and oratorical force – 'the tremendous projectile' was a sobriquet aptly bestowed upon him. But he was uprooted because the Peelites, after the death of their leader in 1850, became a party of high quality but of few numbers, who were in transit from a Tory shore to – probably but not certainly – a Liberal harbour. Gladstone's trouble was that he found almost equally antipathetic the beckoning lights of both the departed shore (in the shape of Disraeli) and the other bank (in the shape of Palmerston). He distrusted them both – so he took some time to make up his mind. This was the reason he did not go to Willis's Rooms. But he eventually decided that Palmerston had at least the advantage of being the older – twenty-five years his senior, whereas Disraeli was only five years so. Gladstone was never a cynic, but he could sometimes act in a way that cynics might regard as well calculated to suit his future political convenience. So in 1859 he formed a 'hostile partnership' with Palmerston under which he was for six years his Chancellor of the Exchequer, disagreeing with him on almost everything, for Palmerston by the 1860s had become a Liberal only in the sense that he believed in keeping the Conservatives out of office. Yet somehow the two jogged along together, with mutual respect mingled with disagreement, with each observing the other's prerogatives, and with Gladstone knowing that Palmerston could not last much longer. When he died, still in office and very old for the period, on the eve of his eight-first birthday, there was a short Russell interregnum until 1867, when Gladstone succeeded to the full leadership, which he was to occupy until 1894, except for the few years of nominal withdrawal in the late 1870s in order to write theology. Yet this withdrawal enhanced rather than diminished his power and indispensability over twenty-seven years and four premierships.

These four premierships were of varying quality. The first was probably the best. It disestablished the Anglican church in Ireland, thus ending the anomaly of the religion of a tiny minority of the population enjoying full state privilege. Gladstone personally remained a passionately committed high Anglican to the end of his life, certainly more religiously committed than any subsequent prime minister except perhaps for Mr Blair, but he moved from a very authoritarian position on religion in his early books to a belief in full tolerance for others. The University Tests Act opened Oxford and Cambridge to dissenters and Roman Catholics. That first government also created the Ballot Act, which even with the limited franchise of less than 3 million was essential to fair as opposed to influenced voting. There was also an Education Act that for the first time provided a national framework of elementary schools to supplement the previous, religion-based system, which had been patchy. Internationally, Britain kept out of the Franco-Prussian War in 1870, and in 1872 accepted the Alabama Award, which involved Britain paying a vast sum in damages (5 per cent of the total budget) to the United States in compensation for the activities of a British built and launched Atlantic raider, which the Confederacy had used during the Civil War to inflict grave damage on Union shipping. This settlement was more than the greatest nineteenth-century triumph of rational internationalism over short-sighted jingoism; it also marked the crucial divide between the previous hundred years of two Anglo-American wars and the twentieth-century habit of close North Atlantic cooperation.

All this, and other, lesser measures, too, added up to a formidable record for a single government. Like nearly all governments, it ended badly, but its five-and-one-quarter years of office made it in many ways the outstanding administration of the century.

Gladstone led three subsequent governments. He was the only man in Britain ever to achieve four separate premierships, and the only one ever to be in office until the age of eighty-four, beating both Palmerston and Churchill – his nearest rivals in this respect – by over three years. But none of these three subsequent governments compared in achievement with the first, although paradoxically he personally became an ever more dominant figure in the country, both loved and hated. The phrase the Grand Old Man, or G.O.M., increasingly used, was coined only in 1881. His last two governments, the one lasting only six months and the fourth no more than twenty, were dominated by Gladstone's conviction that Home Rule (that is, without a separate foreign policy or military independence) was the only solution for Ireland. He arrived at this view by a solitary process of ratiocination over the summer of 1885, a process that involved much study of the Canada Acts of 1840 and of 1867.

He was overwhelmingly right on the issue. There was no other way that the albatross of the Irish problem could be cut from the neck of British politics. But he was not good at presenting this dramatic change of position to his major colleagues. As a result he lost two of them, Hartington, later Duke of Devonshire, from the right of the party and Joseph Chamberlain from the left, while the loyalty of several others was severely strained, though without breaking. The Hartington/Chamberlain defection was enough to defeat the first Home Rule bill (that of 1886) in the House of Commons. The second (that of 1893) got through the Commons by a narrow majority of 34, but foundered in the House of Lords by a crushing majority of 419 to 41. It was one of the most short-sighted votes ever cast in that archaic chamber, the historical sagacity of which is often exaggerated, for with it there disappeared the last hope of Anglo-Irish reconciliation within a common British polity.

And with it too (or very soon afterwards) there disappears from my theme (but certainly not from history) William Ewart Gladstone. He was not necessarily the greatest prime minister – I think I would put Churchill higher because he so matched his hour and succeeded in his central purpose – but Gladstone was certainly the most remarkable specimen of humanity ever to inhabit 10 Downing Street. This was so first because of his phenomenal energy, both physical and mental, which led to his touching life at so many different points. This displayed itself in his climbing Ben Macdhue – an eight-hour round trip – during a visit to Queen Victoria at Balmoral in his seventy-fifth year; and in his engaging with vigour in almost every theological and doctrinal dispute of the late nineteenth century, of which there were many; and in his filling in time, when he was prime minister, by translating the odes of Horace and writing slightly fantastical critiques of Homer, in which he endeavoured to portray him as part of the headwaters of Christianity; and in his claim, surprisingly well authenticated, that he had read 20,000 books – an average of nearly three hundred a year – during his reading lifetime.

And second because of the riveting nature of his oratory, which enabled him to hold great popular audiences spellbound for several hours at a time even when, without amplification, most of them could not easily hear what he was saying, and even when, if they could, it was pretty recondite stuff. His oratory was intensely physical – the flash of his eagle's eye, the swoop of his cadences, the drama of his gestures. It took a physical form that he might have used for perverse purposes, but did not. The Queen thought he might become 'a half-mad dictator' but few others did. He was deeply imbedded in the parliamentary process and gave almost too much respect to his Cabinet colleagues, never sacking them. He believed in an international rule of law, as he showed in the Alabama case, and in the concert of Europe. *Securus judicat ortis terrarum* – the united verdict of the whole world must be accepted as conclusive – was his favourite precept, and mostly it was also his practice.

In spite of all this he did not leave much of an immediate legacy to the Liberal Party. He was never much interested in social reform – or constructive radicalism, as he sceptically called it – which was coming increasingly into fashion at the turn of the century. His immediate successor (although not his choice) for the tail end of that Liberal government of 1892–5 was the 5th Earl of Rosebery, who was perhaps the least satisfactory of all the Liberal prime ministers, despite being a powerful, somewhat florid orator and an elegant literary stylist. But he was extremely selfish, always complaining, and veered off far to the right soon after he left office. Nor was he a nice man. Just as Gladstone was the greatest human being to occupy 10 Downing Street, so Rosebery may well have been the nastiest. But even had he possessed more virtues he probably would not have had a successful premiership. 'Tail-end Charlies' – in other words, those who come in after a long and powerful prime minister of the same party – practically never do. This has been true not only of Rosebery after Gladstone but also of Balfour after Salisbury, Neville Chamberlain after Baldwin, Eden after Churchill, Douglas Home after Macmillan, Callaghan after Wilson, and Major after Thatcher.

After Rosebery had flounced out, the Liberal Party was split into three factions by the South African war, and appeared for half a generation almost as unelectable as Disraeli had made the Conservative Party in the middle of the nineteenth century, and as the Labour Party was made by the defection of Ramsay MacDonald in the 1930s and made itself throughout the 1980s and the beginning of the 1990s. There were only three years of rather hesitant Liberal office between 1886 and 1905.

Then, in the strange way that parties recover, sometimes when they are least expected to do so, the tail end of the long Conservative government provided the Liberals with a number of defensive rather than adventurous issues on which they could come together. Joseph Chamberlain, perhaps the greatest wrecking genius of British politics, having split the Liberals over Home Rule in 1886, proceeded to split the Conservatives over Protection and Imperial Preference in 1903. Balfour equivocated, and the Liberals, fortified by a few Conservative floor-crossing recruits, of whom by far the most notable was twenty-nine-year-old Winston Churchill, rallied to the defence of traditional free trade. A Conservative Education Bill, which, while rather progressive, nonetheless offended the sectarian susceptibilities of the mainly Liberal nonconformists, was another piece of cement for the Liberals.

Sir Henry Campbell-Bannerman, a benign walrus of a man who had been drafted in as leader at the time of greatest schisms, successfully put together a government at the end of 1905, after the Balfour government collapsed, and proceeded to win one of the only three (the others were Labour in 1945 and 1997) left-of-centre landslide majorities in the largely Tory-dominated twentieth century. Campbell-Bannerman was quite a successful if easy-going prime minister for two-and-one-quarter years. He combined a taste for French culture and fashionable German spas with a determined Scottish radicalism. Edward VII paid him the compliment – very high from that self-indulgent gourmand source – of saying that 'Bannerman knows how to order a good dinner in all the best restaurants of Europe.' But from the beginning, the real lynchpin of the government was the Chancellor of the Exchequer, Herbert Henry Asquith, who succeeded effortlessly to the top job when Campbell-Bannerman's health failed in 1908. Bannerman died in 10 Downing Street, the only prime minister to do so, for power is generally speaking a considerable preservative.

Asquith was the last head of a Liberal government. He was a highly educated classicist from a lower-middle-class background, with as natural an aptitude for fashionable life as for the speedy and calm discharge of public business. He did not have the charisma of his distinguished lieutenants Lloyd George and Churchill, but for at least the first six years of his premiership he had the natural authority to remain in reasonable control of them, and the confidence to give them room for plenty of initiatives. He did not have an adventurous mind that breached new frontiers, but he had knowledge, judgment, insight, and tolerance. He was a great peacetime prime minister, and I would place him very high among the nineteen of the twentieth century's, either second or third. Like those other considerable radical prime ministers, Gladstone before him and Attlee (Labour prime minister from 1945 to 1951) afterwards, he was a man of rather conservative, establishment tastes in everything outside politics.

Throughout the Campbell-Bannerman period it did not matter that Home Rule was not proposed, for virtually every controversial bill of the new government – education, licensing (of alcoholic sales), a Scottish land bill – was destroyed by the House of Lords. Until that veto could be limited, the government with the biggest majority in recent history was locked in a vice of impotence.

It was Asquith's great achievement that he loosened that vice. He encouraged Lloyd George, whom he made chancellor when he became prime minister, to take command of the cavalry advance guard in this battle, and Churchill to be his second-in-command. But it was Asquith himself who retained calm control of the central operation, after the two general elections in one year that were necessary to persuade the King that he had no alternative but to agree, if necessary, to create enough new peers to override the massive Conservative majority in the Lords and to replace the absolute veto with a suspensory one of just over two years. This put Home Rule back on the agenda, for although the Liberals had won the two general elections in the sense of leaving the Conservatives in a Commons minority and without allies, they were now dependent on Irish Nationalists and Labour support.

Lloyd George and Churchill, working for a time in close alliance and each always fascinated by the other's streak of political genius, were the so-called heavenly twins of radical social advance. They cut themselves firmly adrift from Gladstonian distrust of state interference in the coalition of the people. Lloyd George produced the so-called People's Budget of 1909, which, although very modest by later standards, was alleged at the time to amount to a several-pronged attack upon property. It was a free trade budget in the sense that it showed how the modestly mounting

costs of social security and Dreadnought bat-
tleships could be paid for without resorting to
import duties. It provoked the Conservative
peers to rashly overextend their battlefront. In
rejecting this budget they were challenging the
doctrine that the Commons had exclusive control over finance, a doctrine that had been per-
ceived as secure for several centuries; in so
doing, they planted themselves on ground that
ensured their defeat in the Parliament Act of
1911. Both Lloyd George and Churchill were
active fighting generals in this battle, although
Asquith remained firmly in the commander-
in-chief's seat. Both were also eager skirmish-
ers for various pieces of social legislation:
health and employment insurance, minimum
standards and wages in the sweated trades, and
the setting up of labour exchanges to reduce
frictional unemployment. All this made
Churchill the sorcerer's apprentice to Lloyd
George's sorcerer (the latter was over eleven
years his senior). It also meant that they had
turned their backs very firmly on the old Gladstonian tradition of concentrating on libertarian political issues and leaving 'the condition of
the people' to look after itself.

Both Churchill and Lloyd George were,

however, never very strong party men, even though they often appeared violently partisan. Lloyd George, who came from a modest but pastoral (and therefore not squalid) North Wales background, was until 1914 seen as a scourge of the prosperous classes. Yet as early as 1910 he had written a memorandum strongly urging a Liberal/Conservative coalition, with a trade-off of advantages for both sides. This had been strongly supported by Churchill, whose background was quite different – he was a duke's grandson and firmly upper-class. That much aside, in those pre-1914 days both were radical opportunists, natural partisans so long as the battle was joined, but always looking out for the opportunity of a favourable truce.

Churchill in those days was even more unpopular with the right than was Lloyd George. Both were seen as noisy firebrands, although Churchill, perhaps because his oratory was less musical, had an even greater capacity to jangle nerves. He was also seen as a class traitor and a turncoat; neither of these epithets was remotely applicable to Lloyd George in his radical days.

Their oratory was remarkably contrasting.

Besides being more musical, Lloyd George's was far more spontaneous; Churchill's was more literary and high-flown and always meticulously prepared. The physical presence of an audience was crucial to Lloyd George, who wrapped himself around his listeners, as it were; for him, a successful speech was an emotional catharsis. Churchill depended far less on an audience. That was one reason why, from the 1920s onwards and above all during the Second World War, he was such a brilliant broadcaster. He could perform as well with only a microphone before him as in front of 2,000 people. Lloyd George could not.

Churchill was nonetheless very successful, even as a young minister – and he started as a full minister when he was thirty-one, the youngest for a century – at creating memorable phrases, which were strongly partisan, anti-Tory, and designed to enthuse the Liberal faithful.

Yet there were always some who doubted whether he ever was a real Liberal. He had of course started as a Tory MP, and by 1924 (and the age of fifty) he was back as a Tory and Chancellor of the Exchequer in a Conservative government. By then the hope of another Lib-

eral government had become very thin. Lloyd
George as prime minister had presided over a
war-winning but largely Tory coalition, and
had continued that alliance, on a still more
Tory base, for the first four years of the peace.
But in so doing, and as a result of his rupture
with Asquith, he had destroyed the Liberal
Party as an instrument of government. And
Churchill was very much interested in govern-
ment as opposed to the sterility of opposition.

But how good a Liberal was he in his
Asquith government days? He certainly
believed in social reform, and during his year-
and-a-half as Home Secretary he was strongly
Liberal on penal policy. He was instinctively
on the side of the underdog, and favoured him
at the expense of the middle dog, especially
provided he himself could remain a top dog.
He was instinctively in favour of a hierarchical
society and did not envisage reforms that
would drastically upset the established social
order. This did not, however, differentiate him
from Gladstone, who pronounced himself to
John Ruskin as a firm inegalitarian. What did
differentiate him from Gladstone was his intui-
tive imperialism and the stimulus that he
derived from the clash of arms. This latter

quality was of crucial benefit to the Western world in 1940, but it was not Gladstonian. Gladstone would have been a rotten war leader, and he was very lucky that his sixty-two years in politics were among the most peaceful in British history.

In Britain any early hope of a future Liberal government perished in the 1920s; but this did not mean that the influence of liberalism disappeared from British politics. Baldwin was a liberal Tory prime minister in the 1920s and 1930s. So was Macmillan in the 1950s. There were considerable liberal influences in both the Labour and Conservative parties. But few Liberal parliamentary seats. In 1983, after new strength was injected into the old Liberal Party through its amalgamation with the short-lived but powerful catalyst the Social Democratic Party, the new alliance got 26 per cent of the popular vote but only 3.5 per cent of the seats.

Any significant recovery in parliamentary seats came only in the 1997 election, when Tony Blair was swept into power with 417 seats, nearly two-thirds of the House of Commons. The Conservatives were reduced to 130, and the Liberal Democrats secured 46 seats, the best Liberal showing in twenty years. But at least half of these 46 seats were gained – as were many of Mr Blair's 417, for he polled only 44 per cent of the popular vote – on the basis of spontaneous cross-voting between Labour supporters and Liberal Democrats. There was no formal pact. There was no withdrawal of candidates in each other's favour. But the electorate, feeling very strongly that the eighteen-year-old Conservative government had far overstayed its welcome, took matters into their own hands and created an unbaptized, almost unacknowledged, popular alliance. When it was thought that the Liberal Democratic candidate was more likely to beat the Conservatives, he or she got Labour support, and vice versa.

This was welcome to Mr Blair, as it was to me and to most Liberal Democrats. It gave him, in a very loose sense, a 62 per cent as opposed to a 44 per cent mandate. What does this hold for the future? Was it purely a one-off phenomenon that will not repeat itself in new circumstances? No one yet knows. The Liberal Democrats mostly support the Labour government rather than the Conservatives, but by no means always.

What is certain is that Mr Blair would like to

see cross-voting continue, would like a strong Liberal/Labour alliance, would like almost a re-creation of the old governing Gladstonian party, thereby avoiding the split on the centre-left of British politics that made the twentieth century overwhelmingly a Conservative century, in a way that the nineteenth century never was and that he and I very much hope the twenty-first century will not be either. He would like all these things more than would much of his party. He has been a strong leader, partly from temperament and partly from his vote-winning ability, which does not yet show great signs of diminution.

This raises the question, how good a Liberal is he? The answer is mixed, but with the positive somewhat predominating. He has certainly rid the Labour Party of much of its old ideological baggage. Far from wanting further nationalization, he has been almost as keen a privatizer as was Mrs Thatcher. He has laid to rest the view that the Labour Party is essentially a class party. He has pursued active policies of constitutional reform much in line with the Liberal tradition, policies that include devolution to Scotland and Wales, the removal of a large part of the hereditary element from the

House of Lords, and the introduction of pro-portional voting systems for the Scottish, Welsh, and London assemblies and for the British members of the European Parliament. But he has so far balked at extending that to the Westminster Parliament, which is a central desire of the Liberal Democrats.

He is also torn between his commitment to decentralize power and his strong desire to maintain centralized control over his own party. This is half understandable, given the mess he thinks his party made of its electoral prospects in the 1980s. But he has not exercised his control at all skilfully, especially in relation to his choice of Labour candidate for the new, directly elected Mayor of London, and of the leader of the Welsh Assembly.

Furthermore, he is not instinctively a Liberal on social libertarian issues. He tends to want to tell people what they ought to do, rather than pull back the law from interference in people's decisions about their own lives and conduct where this does not clearly damage others.

He is, however, instinctively internationalist and pro-European, which is a very important item in the Liberal Democrat creed. He is the most pro-European British prime minister since Edward Heath, who left office twenty-six years ago. I think he wants to see Britain part of a single European currency, but has been hesitant – I think too cautious – about the timing.

So the balance sheet from a Liberal point of view is by no means bad, but not perfect either. But very few things in human life are perfect. Also, it is too early to make full judgments about Mr Blair's prime ministerial performance. It is unwise to tip the waiter before the meal is over. It is unwise to judge a prime minister in the context of history before he has run his course. Mr. Blair has certainly shown himself a competent prime minister. Whether he will be a great one and a true Liberal heir to those others – Gladstone, Asquith, Churchill, and Lloyd George – remains to be seen. But I am not without hope.

Concluding Remarks

Toast to Lord Jenkins

H. GARFIELD EMERSON, QC

Today has been a special treat for me, and I
know for all of us here tonight who have participated in today's series of events.

Lord Jenkins, your lecture was music to the
ears of a graduate of Honours History from
this university, and I enjoyed it tremendously.

The business world currently focuses on the
trading prices of Internet stocks. Lord Jenkins,
you reminded us of the importance of real values in our society – or, in today's parlance,
what I might call 'meaningful content.'

We are most grateful for your presentation
and thoughts today and for your contribution,

not only to the University of Toronto and Victoria University, but also to our community.

Baroness Scotland, your presence and participation with us tonight has been an added and special pleasure for us all. We are most thankful that you have joined us, and we have enjoyed your insights and perspectives that you have shared with us.

As we have several distinguished representatives of the United Kingdom here tonight, and as we share a head of state as well as fundamental traditions and values, it is my pleasure to propose a toast, in light of today's special events, in honour of Her Majesty, Queen Elizabeth.

I hope you will note that the toast was a tribute to her majesty in all her capacities and not just right of Canada.

On special occasions such as today, it is also appropriate to give thanks and to wish for continued progress at Victoria University.

Senator Davey, your endorsement of this annual lecture series in your name has enabled Victoria to attract to our campus distinguished world intellects and speakers such as Lord Jenkins. By virtue of your sponsorship, this university and our community benefit from today's events, and Victoria is most thankful to you and your friends.

Our institution was renamed from Upper Canada Academy to Victoria College in 1841 in honour of Queen Victoria. I doubt the change of name at that time was an attempt to influence Lord Durham's report to her majesty's government on how to deal with Upper and Lower Canada, as we then were.

Baroness Scotland, on your return, you may report to her majesty's government of today that, since Lord Durham's days, it appears that there has been little change with respect to investment matters between Upper and Lower Canada.

The name of our university is, however, a recognizable symbol of our heritage of which we are tremendously proud.

With these thoughts in mind, I am also pleased to ask you to join with me in a toast in honour of Victoria University and its continued progress.

To Victoria University.

Commentary

BARONESS SCOTLAND OF
ASTHAL, QC

Lord Jenkins very cleverly ended his speech by leaving the question – is Tony Blair a liberal? – open. No doubt he hoped I would be able to finish off the subject. I will not do so, I am afraid. But I would say that Tony Blair has redefined politics in Britain, and elsewhere, in the last three years.

The concept of a third way may raise smiles of the 'what does it mean' variety, but I think we have managed to define this government as one that believes in – to use the words of the French prime minister, Lional Jospin – 'a market economy but not a market society.' Does this make us liberal? I'll leave history to judge.

I would like, if I may, to say a few words about the U.K. and Canada.

Canada and Britain share a long history. We pursue the same objectives at home and abroad, and we understand each other instinctively. Both in 1914 and 1939 Canada was the first of Britain's allies to come to its support – support that endured throughout the fighting of two world wars.

Today our armed forces continue to work closely together: 10,000 British troops train in Canada each year. Our troops stand side by side on peacekeeping operations, in Kosovo and East Timor. And it is not just in the armed forces but in all areas that Canadians and Brits find it easy and rewarding to work together.

Lord Jenkins's fascinating talk, and the warm welcome he received, show me how close the links between us are. Shortly after becoming prime minister, Tony Blair said of the relationship between Britain and Canada, and I quote: 'I believe our two countries matter far more to each other than is sometimes recognized. I look forward to strengthening the close ties between us.' In that spirit, our prime ministers set out in 1997 a framework for cooperation to give a fresh impetus to that relationship. This provided for closer cooperation on the international stage, in trade and investment, science and technology, defence, parliamentary contacts, education, and culture. Just last week we saw the Britain–Canada Parliamentary Group, consisting of eight parliamentarians from our three main political parties, visit Canada and share experiences with their Canadian counterparts. A few weeks earlier, Baroness Jay, the Leader of the House of Lords, visited Canada for a series of consultations on women's issues, and David Lock, Minister in the Lord Chancellor's Department met with Canadian experts on legal issues. There is also constant transatlantic collaboration between our officials on a wide range of topics, covering everything from defence and policing to cultural industries and education. Aside from politics and officialdom, there are other hugely important ties.

Both Britain and Canada are multicultural societies, and we value our diversity. A few weeks ago a group of young people from an organization called Tolerance in Diversity, based in the deprived Tower Hamlets area of London, came to Canada as part of Canada's Action 2000 Initiative marking the UN's International Day for the Elimination of Racial Discrimination. They travelled to Saskatchewan and Ottawa swapping their stories and experience with Canadian peers. The friendships they made here will continue – after all, most teenagers are just a mouse click away!

There are tremendous links in education. Chancellor Jackman waxed lyrical about Oxford University earlier today. But I would say that the quad outside Victoria University and the decidedly unscruffy senior common room are the match for many Oxford colleges. Over the past five years the British Council alone has assisted over 150 visits of Canadian researchers and students to Britain and 130 visits of their British counterparts to Canada. This April we begin a significant program of teacher exchanges. We have increased the number of students sent to the U.K. under our Chevening Scholarship program every year for the last three years, and will continue to do so in years to come.

We have a huge trade relationship. Britain is Canada's third-largest trading partner and second-largest direct foreign investor, exporting some £2.5 billion worth of goods in 1998 and £1.1 billion in services. Last year we opened an additional trade office in Calgary and launched an 'Export Canada' drive.

These are but a few examples of the close relations we have. I am honoured to be a part of the exchange today, which is not just a good example of academic linkages between our countries but a signal illustration of the deep intellectual understanding shared by scholars on both sides of the Atlantic. Lord Jenkins, thank you for your elegant and perceptive words. Senator Davey, congratulations on your fine career. Victoria University representatives, thank you for your hospitality, and for your insight in selecting the speaker and in putting together such a worthwhile program.

Biographical Notes

Lord Roy Jenkins

Lord Roy Jenkins, Baron of Pontypool in the County of Gwent, statesman and scholar, has served as Chancellor of Oxford University since 1987 and leader of the Social and Liberal Democratic peers since 1988. He has been President of the Royal Society of Literature since 1988 and co-President of the Royal Institute of International Affairs since 1993.

Born in 1920, Lord Jenkins was educated at University College, Cardiff, and at Balliol College, Oxford, becoming an honorary fellow of the college in 1969. The first leader of the Social Democratic Party in 1982–83, his roots in political activity were laid as a student of philosophy, politics, and economics when he chaired the Oxford University Democratic Socialist Club and the Oxford Union Society.

After serving in the military between 1939 and 1946, he was a staff member of the Industrial and Commercial Finance Corporation Limited. Lord Jenkins was also an adviser to, and director of financial operations of, the John Lewis Partnership and director of Morgan Grenfell Holdings Ltd.

He was elected MP (Labour) for Central Southwark in 1948 and was appointed Principal Private Secretary to the Secretary of State for Commonwealth Relations (1949–50). He later served as Minister of Aviation (1964–65), Home Secretary (1965–67), and Chancellor of the Exchequer (1967–70). Lord Jenkins continued his political career as Deputy Leader of the Labour Party from 1970 to 1972. He was President of the European Community from 1977 to 1981. In 1981 he contested the Glasgow Hillhead riding as the first Social Democratic candidate and was elected in 1982. He acted as the U.K. delegate to the Council of Europe from 1955 to 1957. Among his many activities in the political arena, he served as President of the Britain in Europe Referendum campaign and as President of the United Kingdom Council of the European Movement.

Lord Jenkins has delivered a vast array of brilliant lectures at universities from Harvard to Victoria and in cities from Brussels to Berkeley.

Among his many honours are membership in the American Academy of Arts and Sciences and fellowships at Yale and St Antony's College. He has received honorary degrees from Berkeley, Yale, Oxford, St Antony's, Pennsylvania, Urbino, Kent, Keele, Essex, Open, Leuven, Georgetown, West Virginia, Glamorgan, Bologna, Leeds, Harvard, Dundee, Wales, Loughborough, Glasgow, City, Warwick, Reading, Oxford, Michigan, and Bath.

His books, which include *Mr. Attlee: An Interim Biography*, *Pursuit of Progress*, *Mr. Balfour's Poodle*, *Sir Charles Dilke: A Victorian Tragedy*, *The Labour Case*, *Asquith*, *Afternoon on the Potomac*, *What Matters Now*, *Nine Men of Power*, *Partnership of Principle*, *Truman*, *Gladstone*, *Baldwin*, *Gallery of Twentieth-Century Portraits*, *Portraits and Miniatures*, *European Diary*, and *A Life at the Centre*, have received many literary awards and prizes.

Lord Jenkins, recipient of the Grand Cross, the Legion of Honour of Senegal, the Charlemagne Prize, the Robert Schuman Prize, the Order of European Merit, the Order of Charles III (Spain) and the Order of Infante D. Henrique (Portugal), is currently writing a biography of Churchill.

Lord Jenkins taught Prime Minister Blair at one time and had the opportunity to meet and to work with many of the prime ministers of Great Britain. His work is illuminated not only by his wisdom and great intelligence but also by the warmth of his personality and by a wealth of personal, sagacious, and witty observations.

Senator Keith Davey

Keith Davey was born in Toronto on 21 April 1926 (the same day as Queen Elizabeth), the son of Charles 'Scotty' Minto Davey and Grace Viola Curtis. He attended North Toronto Collegiate Institute, graduating in 1946, and went on to Victoria University, where he received a BA in 1949. He was an excellent student and president of the student council to boot, although in his typically self-deprecating fashion he recalls that at one point his grades were so poor that he had to surrender the Senior Stick. His humility prevents him from noting that the prized honour was awarded to

Senator Keith Davey

the student with the highest grades who also participated actively in campus life.

Following his graduation from university and a brief stint at the Faculty of Law, he went to work for Foster Hewitt and CKFH radio station in sales, rapidly becoming sales manager, a position he would hold for eleven years.

In 1960 he ventured into Canadian politics as campaign organizer for his home riding of Eglinton in Toronto. Having already served as president of Toronto and York's Young Liberal Association, he became national organizer of the Liberal Party in 1961. From 1962 to 1984 he was chair or co-chair of eight national Liberal election campaigns. *Globe and Mail* columnist Scott Young dubbed him 'the Rainmaker' in honour of his ability to precipitate votes for his favourite candidates. Senator Davey would later use this title for his political memoir, *The Rainmaker: A Passion for Politics*, published in 1986.

In 1966 he was appointed to the Senate by Prime Minister Lester B. Pearson. His various contributions there include chairing the important Senate Committee on Mass Media. He worked closely with Prime Ministers Pearson and Pierre Trudeau, offering political advice and sharing warm and loyal friendships.

On his retirement from the upper house in 1996, his colleagues, under the leadership of Senator Jerry Grafstein, raised funds to honour his contribution to Canada and to political life in this country by establishing a lecture series in his honour at Victoria University. Though he retired from the Senate before the required age, he has not left public life; he is still active in politics and in his commitment as a family man, and is an avid sports fan. He is married to Dorothy Elizabeth Speare, and they have three children – Catherine, Douglas, and Ian – eight grandchildren, and countless friends.

Baroness Scotland of Asthal, QC

After graduating with an honours degree in law from London University, Patricia Scotland was called to the bar at the age of twenty-one. She has specialized in family and public law and has chaired or represented parties in a number of major inquiries relating to child abuse, mental health, and housing. She is a member of the Bar of Antigua and the Commonwealth of Dominica. She was appointed a QC and an Assistant Recorder in 1991, and is approved to sit as a Deputy High Court Judge of the Family Division. In 1997 she was made a life peer, taking her seat in the Lords as Baroness Scotland of Asthal.

In addition to playing an active role in several bodies connected with the legal profession, Baroness Scotland has served on a number of bodies dealing with issues such as child abduction, family mediation, racial equality, consumer affairs, the treatment of mentally ill offenders, the BBC World Service, the Millennium, and the Caribbean. She is an honorary Fellow of Wolfson College, Cambridge.

Baroness Scotland was appointed a junior minister at the Foreign and Commonwealth Office in July 1999. Her responsibilities include North America, the Caribbean, and overseas dependent territories; consular affairs and information issues; cultural relations; and personnel matters. In addition, she is responsible for defending the government's foreign policy in the House of Lords.

The Senator Keith Davey Lectures

John Kenneth Galbraith
The Socially Concerned Today
(University of Toronto Press, 1997)

Michael Ignatieff
'The Liberal Imagination:
A Defence'
January 1998

Ruud Lubbers
*Revitalizing Liberal Values
in a Globalizing World*
(University of Toronto Press, 1999)

Lord Roy Jenkins
The British Liberal Tradition
(University of Toronto Press, 2001)